SOCIAL NETWORKING

GLOBAL CITIZENS: SOCIAL MEDIA

Published in the United States of America by Cherry Lake Publishing
Ann Arbor, Michigan
www.cherrylakepublishing.com

Content Adviser: Marcus Collins, MBA, Chief Consumer Connections Officer, Marketing Professor
Reading Adviser: Marla Conn MS, Ed., Literacy specialist, Read-Ability, Inc.

Photo Credits: © Rawpixel.com/Shutterstock.com, Cover, 1; © Monkey Business Images/Shutterstock.com, 5, 10; © Vladimir Sukhachev/Shutterstock.com, 6; © Flamingo Images/Shutterstock.com, 8; © Sergey Novikov/Shutterstock.com, 13; © Robert CHG/Shutterstock.com, 14; © Rades/Shutterstock.com, 17; © thanet007 / Shutterstock.com, 19; © stockphoto mania/shutterstock.com, 20; © Sabphoto/Shutterstock.com, 23; © Trum Ronnarong/Shutterstock.com, 25; © ColorMaker/ Shutterstock.com, 27; © Halfpoint/Shutterstock.com, 28

Library of Congress Cataloging-in-Publication Data

Names: Orr, Tamra, author.
Title: Social networking / Tamra B. Orr.
Description: Ann Arbor : Cherry Lake Publishing, [2019] | Series: Global citizens: social media | Audience: Grade 4 to 6 | Includes bibliographical references and index.
Identifiers: LCCN 2018035579 | ISBN 9781534143043 (hardcover) | ISBN 9781534139602 (pbk.) | ISBN 9781534140806 (pdf) | ISBN 9781534142008 (hosted ebook)
Subjects: LCSH: Online social networks—Juvenile literature. | Social media—Juvenile literature.
Classification: LCC HM742 .O67 2019 | DDC 302.30285—dc23
LC record available at https://lccn.loc.gov/2018035579

Cherry Lake Publishing would like to acknowledge the work of the Partnership for 21st Century Learning.
Please visit www.p21.org for more information.

Printed in the United States of America
Corporate Graphics

ABOUT THE AUTHOR

Tamra Orr is the author of more than 500 nonfiction books for readers of all ages. A graduate of Ball State University, she now lives in the Pacific Northwest with her family. When she isn't writing books, she is either camping, reading, or on the computer researching the latest topic.

TABLE OF CONTENTS

CHAPTER 1
History: A Need to Belong **4**

CHAPTER 2
Geography: We're All Online **12**

CHAPTER 3
Civics: For the People, by the People **16**

CHAPTER 4
Economics: Businesses on Social Media **22**

THINK ABOUT IT 30
FOR MORE INFORMATION 31
GLOSSARY 32
INDEX 32

CHAPTER 1

History: A Need to Belong

People are different. They look different, speak different languages, and like (and dislike) different things. You're even different from your family and friends. Maybe you think pineapple on pizza should be outlawed, but your brother always orders Hawaiian pizza with extra pineapple. Perhaps you love camping and your friend prefers hotels.

But people are also very much the same. They need the same things—air, water, food, and somewhere to live. They also need something else: to belong. People want to feel connected. It's a basic human drive. Think about how you feel when you are laughing

According to researchers, our need to belong is so fundamental that even one instance of being excluded can affect our health, self-control, and even test performance!

with a friend or having an important conversation with someone in your family. It's a great feeling to be connected. This is why social networking took the world by storm. What started as a chance to chat with others online has turned into one of the most common and popular ways for people to communicate and connect.

AIM was so popular that by the mid-2000s, its users made up over half (52 percent) of the online instant messaging industry!

Reaching Out Online

In the 1970s, computer techies—long before they were known by that term—created **bulletin board systems**. These online meeting places allowed people to chat on a public **forum**. They mainly used it to buy and sell things. It ran through the telephone lines. Because telephone companies charged for all non-local ("long distance") calls at that time, most people just connected with people who lived nearby. In the late 1980s, CompuServe, a system originally designed for businesses to use, went public, and thousands of people began connecting on many different forums.

AOL

In 1985, America Online, or AOL, entered the market. AOL started as an online forum for people who owned outdated Commodore 64 computers. Millions of people became members of the online forum. They filled out their profiles and connected with friends. In the late 1990s to early 2000s, AOL Instant Messenger (AIM) took the nation by storm. AIM wasn't the world's first instant-messaging platform, but it was the most popular. By the mid-2000s, 52 percent of instant messengers were AIM users.

Social Networking Timeline

Company	Launch Year
CompuServe	1980s
AOL (America Online)	1985
Classmates.com	1995
Friendster	2002
LinkedIn; Myspace	2003
Facebook; Twitter	2006
Instagram	2010
Google+; Snapchat	2011
Musical.ly	2014
TikTok	2016

Ryze is similar to LinkedIn in that they both are social networks for business professionals.

Steep Competition

By 2000, AOL was the biggest internet provider in the country. But AIM, the company's early "social network" feature, had a great deal of competition. In 1995, Classmates.com was launched. It was a website focused on connecting people who had attended the same schools. Shortly after that, in the late 1990s and early 2000s, sites like SixDegrees, Ryze, Friendster, and LinkedIn launched. But few had the success that AIM did.

In 2003, Myspace launched. From 2005 to early 2008, it was the leader in social networking. Myspace allowed users to personalize their profiles through features like embedding music and videos into this "space." At its peak in early 2008, the site attracted about 75.9 million visitors! But by April 2008, Facebook had taken over Myspace's number one spot. Twitter also quickly gained popularity. By the early 2010s, AIM's following declined as well. AIM officially signed off the internet for good on December 15, 2017.

According to a study, the top five platforms people spend time on are YouTube, Facebook, Snapchat, Instagram, and Twitter.

Modern Day

Currently, Facebook has more than 2 billion users worldwide. Sites like Snapchat, Instagram, and Twitter are not far behind. Social networking has become a part of many people's daily lives. People check their smartphones between 35 and 150 times a day (depending on the owner's age). The average person spends 2 hours a day on social media—the equivalent of 5 years and 4 months over a lifetime! That is more time than the typical person spends eating, drinking, socializing, and **grooming** all put together.

Developing Questions

There are four types of **textual evidence** *people use when writing a paper or forming an opinion. These are: paraphrases, summaries, references, and quotes. Many people like to use quotes. A quote can have great impact, especially if it's by a powerful public figure. For example, this is a quote by author David Amerland: "Social media is addictive precisely because it gives us something which the real world lacks: it gives us immediacy, direction, and value as an individual."*

Here is a different quote, by politician Anthony Carmona: "Social media websites are no longer … creating a positive communication link among friends, family, and professionals. It is a **veritable** *battleground, where insults fly . . . damaging lives, destroying self-esteem, and a person's sense of self-worth."*

How do these quotes impact you? Do you agree more with Amerland or with Carmona? Why?

CHAPTER 2

Geography: We're All Online

The drive to connect and communicate is not limited to any single type of person or place. This is why many countries have their own social networks specific to their country. Let's take a closer look!

China

Since 2005, the social networking site QZone has been gaining popularity, especially throughout China. It offers its more than 635 million users the ability to blog, customize websites, and share photos and videos. The second-most popular social media platform in China is Weibo. This social network features a character limit for posts—it's like China's version of Twitter. (Twitter, like many other social media platforms, is banned in China.) Renren, another popular social platform in China, is known as "everyone's network."

Less than half the population in France, Greece, and Japan use social media!

Russia

The most popular website in Russia and number nine in the world is VKontakte, or VK. *VKontakte* is a Russian word that means "in touch." The platform launched in 2006 and, like Facebook, emphasizes connecting with friends. The social network is popular in Ukraine, Belarus, and Kazakhstan and has 100 million users. VK's top competitor is Odnoklassniki, which also launched in 2006. It's a platform that relies heavily on photos and video content.

According to a study, about 7 out of 10 people in Sweden, the Netherlands, and Australia use social networking platforms like Facebook and Twitter.

Around the Globe

While Twitter is popular in the United States, it dominates in Japan. The social platform is also people's first choice in parts of the United Kingdom and Europe, as well as Pakistan, Argentina, and the Philippines. In Iran, people use Facenama, which is similar to Facebook. People in Spain and Argentina use Taringa. Taringa is like a combination of Twitter and Reddit, which features news and discussions. In parts of Africa, the leading social networking site is LinkedIn, a business and career social platform that is also popular in the United States. In Botswana, Namibia, Indonesia, and Mozambique, Instagram takes the lead.

Gathering and Evaluating Sources

One of the best ways to learn what makes a social network successful is to look at the ones that have either failed or evolved into something different. For example, Myspace is still around, but now it's for musicians and bands that want to play their latest songs to fans and agents. In 2016, it listed almost 160 million monthly users. Research a few other social networks. Did these platforms evolve? Did they get purchased? Just disappear? Analyze what you find, and then evaluate what you believe makes a social networking site succeed and grow—or phase out.

Civics: For the People, by the People

Social networking makes it possible to follow, respond to, and comment directly to everyone—from celebrities and experts to CEOs and politicians. Before, you might have sent a letter to a politician or were placed on hold just to talk to someone who isn't in charge. Now, you can reach out and send an immediate message to all your local, state, and national representatives. You can also directly complain to or compliment a business and know that the company (and the rest of the world) read your message. This has changed politics, government, and businesses in profound ways.

According to analysts, companies are more likely to respond to a complaint on social media if it were about a product or policy.

Getting Involved

The power of being able to reach out to anyone in the world has revolutionized our means of communication. Tweets, live-stories, hashtags, memes, and posts let companies, celebrities, and politicians know what the public's opinion is concerning their products or behavior. These public figures now have no choice but to learn how to use the different social media platforms to make their announcements, explain decisions, respond to comments, answer questions, and, for politicians, gather votes.

Former president Barack Obama kept in touch with the American people through Twitter. But most Americans know far more about President Donald Trump because of his frequent tweets. He has used Twitter to share his thoughts and ideas more than any other president in history. In return, he gets millions of followers who agree and disagree with him.

Three of Obama's tweets in 2017 made it to Twitter's top 10 most retweeted tweets list.

Free Speech or Fake News?

Social networks are not without flaws. These problems often result in laws being put into effect. Posting a news story in real time is amazing, but what happens if that information turns out to be untrue? "Fake news," or untrue stories published as fact, can spread like wildfire. Studies indicate that lies tend to spread much faster than the truth on social media sites. The impact of this was seen during the 2016 presidential election when, according to sources, Russia created a number of fake social media accounts to try to influence the election.

Make sure to read the social network's terms of use and policy. You might be able to retweet a tweet, repin on Pinterest, or reshare a friend's post, but that doesn't mean you can repost on Instagram!

The problems only expand from there. What would you do, for example, if someone posted a photo of you online and said you were cheating? You know it's not true, but the photo and message have already been tweeted, retweeted, liked, hearted, and shared. The legal term for this is called **libel**. It is illegal in the United States to **defame** someone's character in a way that hurts or ruins their reputation. Whose responsibility is it to remove the post? Should Twitter, Facebook, or Instagram be legally required to take it down? If it were on Snapchat, does it matter that the message will disappear in 24 hours? In Germany, putting altered photos or false claims about someone on social media sites can cause these sites to be fined millions of dollars. This is thanks to the Network Enforcement Act. Yet many believe this law hurts people and platforms more than it protects them.

Social networking is changing the world, as well as politics, governments, and people's rights. It's making it easier and faster to communicate and connect with everyone, from your friend on the next block to the president in the White House.

Developing Claims and Using Evidence

If you hear the word "argument," do you imagine people yelling at each other? Do you picture angry comments and nasty insults? Not all arguments are like this. In writing, speech, and debate, it simply means taking a stance on an issue, developing a claim about it, and then finding evidence to support it. For example, one argument some people have about social networking is that it is not the same as face-to-face socializing. They claim online connections are inferior to in-person connections. Create your own argument on this topic, make a claim, and then gather evidence to support that claim.

CHAPTER 4

Economics: Businesses on Social Media

Every time you post your opinions on politics, fashion, the weather, or products, you are telling the world what you want, need, and are willing to pay for. And that information spreads further the more you post, comment, repost, or retweet. This information helps businesses.

Social Media Impact

Social media has made a huge impact on the economy. Before, you might have gone inside a **brick-and-mortar** store to try on or purchase a sweater you saw advertised in a magazine or

Data shows that there are over 16 million Google searches for "Instagram" per month!

newspaper. Now, you can explore the company's website, read customer reviews, and ask for people's opinion on social media before deciding if you want to purchase the sweater. You may have also seen the sweater you wanted from a **promoted post** or from an **influencer** you're following on social media.

A survey found that 31 percent of people use social media to browse products they're interested in buying. And 66 percent of 18- to 34-year-olds admitted that they look at images of clothing and fashion on social media platforms to inspire them to make

By the Numbers

In every single minute of 2016, more than 30 million messages were posted on Facebook and 350,000 tweets were sent. Fifty-two trillion words are written every day on social media. That is the equivalent of about 520 million books!

As of August 2017, there were 800 million active users on Instagram!

a purchase. Advertisers are taking advantage of this. In fact, since Facebook Ads launched in 2005, the social network giant had reached $9.16 billion in ad sales in early 2017! Also, a little over 70 percent of U.S. businesses, or about 21 million, are on Instagram. This means that many businesses find real value in advertising on social networking platforms.

Entrepreneurs Rejoice

Small business owners and **entrepreneurs** have greatly benefited from social networking platforms. When social media plays a major role in advertising, a big advertising budget is unnecessary. Getting the word out and promoting products or services is easier, reaches an almost unlimited audience, and prevents having to advertise in multiple publications.

Businesses use social media platforms to find and connect with their audience, analyze their social media activity, and build authority in their **niche**. Today's businesses are easier to find,

Communicating Conclusions

Before you read this book, how much time did you spend on social media? Share what you have learned about how people use it to communicate with others. Analyze the following questions. Does using social media meet certain needs for you? Do you find you use social media to keep in touch with friends, family, and other people? How do those connections compare to those you have face-to-face?

According to research, Facebook and Google control over half (57.6 percent) of the digital advertising market!

In 2017, social networks generated about $41 billion from advertising, games, and apps featured on their platforms.

thanks to their online presence. In fact, 82 percent of marketing experts believe that social media impacts brand awareness. These experts also agree that social networks have a significant impact on sales.

Social networking has changed almost everything about modern life. It has changed how you get the news, how you shop, how you get involved with the world, and mostly, how you communicate. Social media gives you the chance to connect with your friends, family, and the entire world. It has truly revolutionized the way people lead their lives today.

Taking Informed Action

There are countless small companies and individuals on the internet who are hoping to grow a business. Spend some time exploring their websites and what they have to offer. How do their websites compare to others who have been in the same business longer? Take a moment to leave helpful feedback on those businesses' social media platforms.

Think About It

It is clear that social media is very important to many people. How hard would it be for some people to give it up entirely? According to a 2018 survey, it depends on who you ask. Overall, about 40 percent of people said it would be difficult, but how difficult largely depended on age. For example, slightly over half of the people between 18 and 24 reported that it would be hard, while only a third of the people over the age of 50 felt that way. (Interestingly, in 2014, when the same survey was done, only 28 percent of social media users overall reported they would have a hard time.) What do all of these numbers indicate about what is happening with social media users? What are some conclusions you can draw based on this information? How hard would it be for you to stop using social media?

For More Information

FURTHER READING

Edwards, Claire. *Social Media and Mental Health: Handbook for Teens.* Tampa, FL: Trigger, 2018.

Lombardo, Jennifer. *Social Networking: Staying Safe in the Online World.* New York: Lucent Press, 2017.

McKee, Jonathan. *The Teen's Guide to Social Media . . . and Mobile Devices: 21 Tips to Wise Posting in an Insecure World.* Uhrichsville, OH: Shiloh Run Press, 2017.

Minton, Eric. *Social Networking and Social Media Safety.* New York: PowerKids Press, 2014.

Richards, Patti. *All about Social Networking.* Lake Elmo, MN: Focus Readers, 2017.

WEBSITES

Kidzworld
www.kidzworld.com
Meet new friends on this social network platform that's designed with kids in mind.

Neopets
www.neopets.com
Keep your pet alive and chat with friends from all over the world while learning basic coding and economics.

GLOSSARY

brick-and-mortar (BRIK AND MOR-tur) a traditional store or business that is in a building instead of on the internet

bulletin board systems (BUL-ih-tin BORD SIS-tuhmz) online collections of electronic messages, posted by and accessible to users

defame (dih-FAME) to injure or destroy someone's reputation

entrepreneurs (ahn-truh-pruh-NURZ) people who organize, manage, and assume the risks of a business

forum (FOR-uhm) an online meeting place for discussions of various topics

grooming (GROOM-ing) making oneself neat or tidy, tending to appearance and clothing

influencer (IN-floo-en-sur) a person on social media who has many followers and has an impact on a specific audience

libel (LYE-buhl) something spoken, written, or drawn that injures a person's good name

niche (NICH) a specialized market or audience

promoted post (pruh-MOTE-id POHST) a post on social media that is promoted by an influencer or company and serves as an advertisement for a product or service; also known as a sponsored post

textual evidence (TEKST-yoo-uhl EV-ih-duhns) text that supports an idea, answers a question, or makes a claim

veritable (VER-ih-tuh-buhl) a word used to emphasize the correctness of a description

INDEX

advertising, 24–29
AIM, 6, 7, 9
AOL (American Online), 7, 9

China, 12
civics, 16–21
connectedness, 4–5

economics, 22–29

Facebook, 7, 9, 10, 13, 15, 20 24
- advertising, 25, 27
- geography, 14

fake news, 19–21
forums, 6, 7

geography, 12–15
Google, 7, 23, 27

influencers, 24
Instagram, 7, 10, 15, 20, 23, 25
instant messaging, 6, 7

libel, 20
LinkedIn, 7, 8, 9, 15

Myspace, 7, 9, 15

Obama, Barack, 18, 19

Russia, 13, 19
Ryze, 8, 9

smartphones, 10
Snapchat, 7, 10, 21
social networking
- advertising, 24–29
- for business people, 8
- civics, 16–21
- early sites, 9
- economics, 22–29
- failures, 15
- geography, 12–15
- history, 4–11
- impact, 22–29
- importance to people, 30
- problems, 19–21
- statistics, 10–11
- timeline, 7
- top platforms, 10

Trump, Donald, 18
Twitter, 7, 9, 10, 12, 20
- geography, 14, 15
- presidents' use of, 18–19

YouTube, 10